Understanding

SEX

Dr Lynne Low

Published by Family Doctor Publications
in association with the British Medical Association

IMPORTANT

This book is intended not as a substitute for personal medical advice
but as a supplement to that advice for the patient who wishes to
understand more about his or her condition.

Before taking any form of treatment YOU SHOULD ALWAYS CONSULT
YOUR MEDICAL PRACTITIONER.

In particular (without limit) you should note that advances in medical
science occur rapidly and some of the information about drugs and
treatment contained in this booklet may very soon be out of date.

© Family Doctor Publications 1997–2004
Updated 1999, 2001, 2003, 2004

Family Doctor Publications, PO Box 4664, Poole, Dorset BH15 1NN

Medical Editor: Dr Tony Smith
Cover Artist: Dave Eastbury
Medical Artist: Philip Wilson
Illustrator: Alex Harwood
Design: MPG Design, Blandford Forum, Dorset
Printing: Nuffield Press, Abingdon, using acid-free paper

ISBN: 1 898205 89 2

Contents

Introduction

Almost everybody has some kind of problem with sex. On the one hand, sex is a biological function, just as eating is. On the other it has the force to be truly life-changing.

Sex may be deeply fulfilling and wildly uplifting, but it also has the power to wreak the greatest psychological, emotional and physical damage. Sex may seal the beginning of a significant relationship, the conception of a much wanted – or much dreaded – pregnancy, or result in 'punishment' in the form of a sexual infection. The drive to seek sexual fulfilment is as natural as hunger for food, but it is often burdened with guilt, anxiety and ignorance.

The deeply personal nature of sex is at odds with the endless coverage in the media. One may have been brought up to be wary and inhibited about sex, yet the pressure to be a full sexual being is great in today's more permissive society. Not only that; many more traditional cultures and religions have strict prohibitive rules about sex, and yet place great emphasis on marriageability and fertility – both central aspects of one's sexual identity.

No wonder we place such great importance on sex, whether we see it primarily as an expression of intimacy or a means of procreation. No wonder we have such high expectations of sex, and of ourselves in sexual roles. And no wonder we may have difficult, unresolved feelings about sex, and find sexual problems so threatening.

It used to be thought that all sexual problems required lengthy, complicated forms of therapy. Now, however, it is known that many sexual difficulties are easy to treat, and often respond very well to simple exercises that can be done at home. Sex therapists find that most of their work is very rewarding. More importantly, couples who have been struggling for some time are greatly relieved by the real improvement they can experience, when they finally get help.

So where do people go for help? If you feel able to confide in your GP, he or she may be a useful source of information and support, and refer you on to psychosexual therapists if necessary. For a more confidential service, genitourinary medicine clinics (sexual health or special clinics) also sometimes run sexual difficulties clinics and would certainly be able to put you in touch with appropriate help.

For direct access to psychosexual counselling and treatment you may contact Relate. The Family Planning Association (UK) can also put you in touch with local help. In London, London Marriage Guidance runs sexual problems clinics. For problems with erections, there is a Sexual Dysfunction Association helpline. All the addresses and telephone numbers are given at the end of the book (see page 76). Specific addresses and helplines are also given for other specific problems.

This book hopes to provide some insight into why the common sex problems occur, and to give some indication as to the kind of therapy available, and how successful this may be. It is not meant to be a do-it-yourself form of treatment, although some couples may find it helpful to adapt some of the exercises described. Instead, the aim is to help couples get a better understanding of the physical and psychological causes of sexual difficulties, and to appreciate how often one leads to another, and a vicious cycle is begun. In this way, the emotional impact of such problems may be eased and, armed with more information, the couple may be in a more articulate and therefore better position to seek help.

KEY POINTS

✓ It is natural to feel threatened by sexual problems

✓ Couples should seek help early

✓ Many GPs, sexual health doctors and relationship counsellors are used to talking about sex problems

✓ Use this book to understand the problem more, but seek professional help

The basic facts

THE MALE SEX ORGANS

The male sex organs consist of the penis and the two testicles, contained in a bag of skin called the scrotum. The penis becomes erect during sexual excitement, and allows penetration of the female vagina, while the testicles produce the male sex hormone, testosterone, and also sperm for fertilising the female egg, the ovum.

The penis

The shaft of the penis is made up of three long tubes of spongy tissue – two identical ones that run on the top side of the penis, each called a corpus cavernosum (plural corpora cavernosa), and another, along the underside of the penis, called the corpus spongiosum. The corpus spongiosum contains the urethra, which is the tube through which urine and semen pass.

At the tip of the penis, the corpus spongiosum expands to form the mushroom-shaped head of the penis called the glans. This is covered by a layer of loose skin called the foreskin. This is removed in circumcised males. A shallow groove lies between the glans and shaft. A delicate fold of skin called the frenum connects the foreskin to the glans, on the underside of the penis. A ring of little spots may appear all round the bottom of the glans, in late adolescence and early adulthood. These are called pearly papules and, although they may cause concern in a young man and be mistaken for warts, they are natural and harmless.

At the base of the penis, there are muscles which contract rhythmically during orgasm, and also have a role to play in erection.

The testicles

The testicles in a male fetus develop in the abdomen, and migrate down into the scrotum only during late

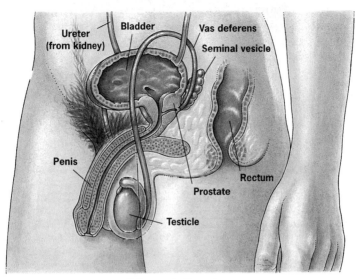

Male reproductive system.

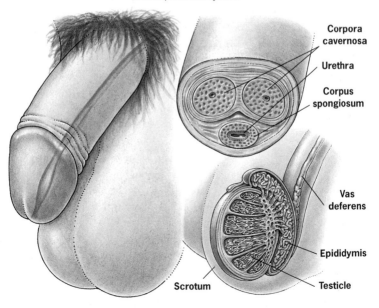

The male sex organs.
Top right: cross-section of penis. Bottom right: cross-section of testicle.

pregnancy. Sometimes this fails to happen, and a small operation is needed during childhood to fix the testicles in the scrotum.

The testicles contain two types of cells – one for producing the male hormone testosterone, the other for sperm production. Sperm passes from the testicles into a collection of tubes bunched together to form the epididymis, which sits like a cap on the top back end of each testicle. From there they pass into another tube called the vas deferens. This is the tube that is cut and tied during a vasectomy, for sterilisation.

The vas deferens leads to an area just behind the bladder where it expands to form a storage area for sperm. Two small glands called the seminal vesicles open into the vas deferens – these produce seminal fluid which forms, together with sperm and fluid from the prostate, the semen that is ejaculated during orgasm. Other glands also open near this area, and they produce a clear fluid which is sometimes discharged early on in sexual arousal and may contain enough sperm to cause pregnancy.

The vas deferens then enters the prostate gland, which sits at the base of the bladder, and there it joins the urethra, the tube that runs along the penis, and that carries urine and semen.

There are two muscles that support the testicles – the dartos muscle causes shrinkage or relaxation of the scrotum, and the cremaster lifts the testicle when it contracts. This muscle can sometimes be overactive in a young man, causing an aching pain in the testicle and groin during arousal and ejaculation. The treatment sometimes prescribed is masturbation in a warm bath.

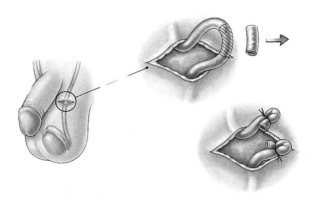

A man may be sterilised by a vasectomy.

THE FEMALE SEX ORGANS

The female sex organs are more complicated than the male sex organs. Internally, in the lower abdomen, sit the uterus or womb, the fallopian tubes and the left and right ovaries. The lower end of the uterus forms the cervix, which juts into the top end of the vagina. The vagina opens out into the external organs, which include the urethra, the clitoris and the vulva.

The clitoris

The clitoris is in many ways a tiny penis. It has the same basic structure of the three tubes along its length and, when a woman is aroused, it also swells and becomes stiff. It is extremely sensitive to touch, being packed with nerve endings, and although women become sexually aroused by stimulation of the clitoris, movements that are too heavy or clumsy can be painful.

The vulva

This consists of two layers of skin: the outer, thicker, labia majora and the inner, more delicate, labia minora. These normally lie against each other to seal the vaginal opening, but if they are parted they reveal the vaginal opening. In a woman who has never had intercourse, or used tampons, a thin membrane of skin called the hymen surrounds this opening making it even smaller. Rarely the hymen may block the vagina altogether, leading to the retention of blood when the girl starts to menstruate. A small operation to cut the hymen is then needed. In other women, the hymen is torn, and hymenal remnants lie around the opening, which may give the vagina a slightly ragged appearance. Sitting in a small bud of tissue just above the vaginal opening, inside the labia minora, is the opening of the urethra, for the passage of urine.

At the bottom of the vaginal opening are two glands, one on each side, called Bartholin's glands. These produce a fluid which lubricates the vagina during intercourse. Sometimes they become infected or swell to form a cyst, and antibiotics or a small operation is necessary.

The vagina

The vagina is shaped like a tube and is normally around 10 centimetres in length. The lower part of the vagina, near the vulva, is bounded by strong muscles which must be relaxed for comfortable penetration. On the other hand, if they become too lax, perhaps after child-bearing, sex may feel less pleasurable for both the man and the woman, and special exercises need to be done to regain the muscle tone.

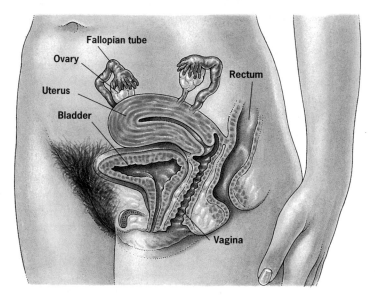

The female sex organs.

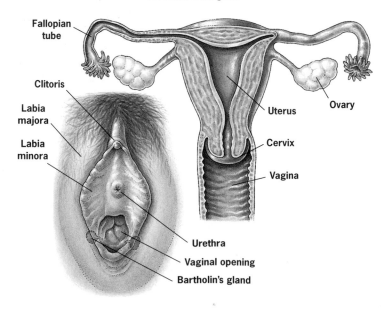

Left: the vulva or external female sex organs; right: the internal female sex organs.

The cervix, or neck of the womb, juts into the upper end. When a cervical or 'pap' smear is done, the cervix is exposed with the help of an instrument called a speculum, to open the vagina, and a small sample of tissue and mucus from the cervix is gently removed and spread on to a slide to be viewed under a microscope. Most women find direct pressure to the cervix uncomfortable, as is repeated buffeting by the penis during sexual intercourse.

The walls of the vagina are corrugated. When a woman is sexually aroused, the upper two-thirds of the vagina increase in size to accommodate the penis fully.

The uterus

The uterus or womb is triangular in shape, with the tip pointing downwards, as the cervix, into the vagina. In most women, the body of the uterus is bent slightly forward and flops over the bladder in front of it. In other women it flops backwards – this is usually of no consequence, except that the position of the cervix may then be tricky to find for a smear! At each upper end, two short arms, called the fallopian tubes, fan out. Finger-like tissue, at the ends of each fallopian tube, encircle one ovary on each side. When a women is sterilised, the fallopian tubes are cut and tied or clipped.

The uterus mainly consists of muscle, and its function is to hold a developing fetus through pregnancy, and then expel it by muscular contractions at labour. Its ability to expand during pregnancy is remarkable, changing from a capacity of six millilitres to four litres in nine months. It is normally only about seven centimetres long.

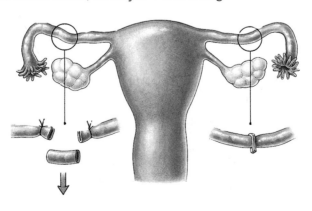

Female sterilisation: the fallopian tube is tied (left) or clipped (right).

Under the influence of hormones, the lining of the uterus builds up each month. If a pregnancy does not occur, this is shed as a woman's period, or menstruation, at the end of the cycle of build up, on average every 28 days. Women's monthly cycles vary a great deal, however, and many women do not have completely regular periods.

If a pregnancy does occur, the lining of the uterus continues to build up, in preparation for the fetus, which will fix itself onto the lining and start to develop. A missed period is therefore often the first sign a woman has that she may be pregnant.

The ovaries

The ovaries contain the eggs, or ova. Each egg is surrounded by a cluster of cells. Each month one egg 'ripens', and the cells around it grow until, at ovulation, the egg breaks through the surface of the ovary and gets taken up by the finger projections of the fallopian tube. It travels down the tube, where, if there are sperm, fertilisation or conception takes place. Ovulation normally takes place 14 days after the start of a woman's period.

WHAT HAPPENS DURING LOVEMAKING?

Foreplay or loveplay is the time that couples spend kissing, cuddling and physically stimulating each other so that they are both ready for intercourse. People vary a lot in the amount of foreplay they like to get them 'in the mood' for sex. Most couples develop a 'routine' that works for both of them, but it is fun occasionally to change this routine, so that intercourse is interspersed with periods of foreplay or oral sex, and new positions are tried. There are no set patterns about what goes on during lovemaking, and no rules that kissing leads to foreplay, which leads to intercourse – making it up as you go along is part of the pleasure.

Kissing (on the lips, body or genitals), cuddling, gentle biting and stroking each other help a couple relax and feel physically close. As they become more aroused, they may start to explore each other's bodies. Women usually enjoy having their breasts and nipples gently stroked or kissed, and their thighs caressed. They may enjoy having a finger or two gently introduced into the vagina. The clitoris is very sensitive, and it may be painful to touch if the woman is not sufficiently aroused, or if the touch is too heavy or rough. Most women enjoy having the shaft (or side) of the clitoris gently and repetitively stroked or patted, and many women find oral sex very exciting.

Men enjoy having the shaft and head of their penis held and stroked repetitively, or kissed, licked and sucked (like an ice cream). They vary in how tightly or loosely they like to be gripped. Some men also enjoy it if their testicles are touched or held, or the buttocks and thighs caressed. Men's nipples are less sensitive than women's, but some men like to have them stimulated as well.

When a couple feel ready for intercourse, the penis is inserted into the vagina and the couple move together, rhythmically, so that their sexual pleasure is increased. For men, the change from stimulation by hand to intercourse usually greatly increases their sexual arousal, but this is not always the case for women. In a loving relationship, women find penetration deeply emotionally satisfying, but positions adopted in intercourse do not always allow for adequate clitoral stimulation. Less experienced women, and women who do not have sex often, may also find penetration uncomfortable, even if they are aroused. Couples need to experiment with various positions to see which ones they can adapt for their own lovemaking.

POSITIONS FOR INTERCOURSE

Many books provide helpful instructions on the seemingly endless positions a couple can adopt for sex, but they are mostly variations of four basic positions, and sometimes require unrealistic degrees of athleticism!

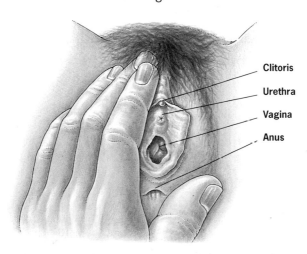

Clitoris

Urethra

Vagina

Anus

The clitoris is very sensitive and may be painful if the touch is too heavy or rough.

Missionary position.

● **The missionary position:** In this position the man rolls on top of the woman with his legs together and inserts his penis into her vagina. The woman lies on her back with her thighs wide enough apart to allow comfortable penetration. The advantage of this position is that the couple can kiss and stroke each other's faces, the man can stroke the woman's breasts, but clitoral stimulation may not be adequate unless the man specifically rubs his penis against the clitoris. Variations of this position include the woman bringing her knees up against her chest, or the man kneeling on the floor with the woman lying half on the bed, with her legs around his waist.

● **Woman on top:** The man lies down on his back and the woman lowers herself onto his penis, sitting astride him. This position is popular with some women who find they

Woman on top.

Side by side.

are more in charge of the frequency and depth of penetration, and can achieve good clitoral stimulation. It is also a good position during pregnancy. The woman may kneel over the man, leaning forward or actually sit on top of him as on a low chair, with her legs in front of her. The couple face each other and the man can stroke the woman's breasts or clitoris. Variations include both partners sitting up cross-legged, the woman with her legs wrapped around the man's waist.

● **Side by side:** Both partners lie on their side facing each other, the woman draws her uppermost leg up, and the man inserts his penis this way. This position allows for prolonged intercourse because both partners are lying down. The couple can stimulate each others' genitals or nipples.

● **Penetration from behind:** Usually the woman kneels on all fours on the bed and the man penetrates her, pushing his body against her buttocks. The man can stroke his partner's back, and play with her breasts and clitoris. The drawback is that partners do not face each other in this position. Variations include a sitting position (the woman sitting on top of the man but facing away from him), or standing up leaning over a bed or table for support.

Penetration from behind.

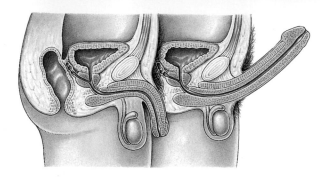

The penis, on the left, in resting position and, on the right, during an erection.

WHAT HAPPENS TO THE BODY DURING INTERCOURSE?

When a man is sexually aroused, his penis becomes erect. Blood flow to the penis increases, and at the same time blood flow *out* of the penis shuts down. The spongy tissue in the two corpora cavernosa and the corpus spongiosum therefore fill with blood and become stiff and hard. The small muscles at the base of the penis also rhythmically contract to maintain the erection.

As stimulation increases, sexual excitement increases and the man becomes aware that orgasm is approaching. He reaches a stage of 'ejaculatory inevitability', when ejaculation occurs within one to three seconds. Muscles in the testicles and the vas deferens contract, ready to pump the semen down the urethra. The passage of urine into the urethra is blocked off. Fluid from the prostate gland and the seminal vesicles mixes with the sperm to form semen, which collects at the top of the urethra. When orgasm arrives, this is propelled down the urethra by muscular action and spurts out of the penis.

After orgasm, there is a period in which a man becomes unresponsive to sexual stimulation. This is called the refractory period and varies from person to person, from minutes to hours. The penis loses its rigidity, the rest of the body relaxes, and often there is a strong desire to sleep.

In a woman, sexual arousal causes swelling of the clitoris and vulva, and increased lubrication. The whole 'introitus', as the opening of the vagina is called, responds in this way to make penile entry easy and pleasurable for the woman. The uterus also increases in size and rises, pulling the cervix out of the way of the penis. The upper part of the vagina balloons. During orgasm the muscles of the vagina and uterus contract rhythmically, and some women also ejaculate a small amount of fluid from the urethra, which is not urine. This is thought to be the female equivalent of male ejaculation. Women do not strictly have a refractory period, and some women are able to have several orgasms in a row.

MALE AND FEMALE SEXUALITY

It is clear from the above descriptions that physical changes during sexual excitement facilitate intercourse in both sexes. Many sexual problems arise because of a couple's different rates and patterns of response, or ability to respond at all. If a man is unable to become aroused and erect, his partner feels sexually frustrated, unattractive and rejected. If a woman is sexually disinterested, she may avoid sex, or complain that it is painful because she is not sufficiently aroused. Her partner may be at a loss to excite her and feel like a failure.

It has been said that men get turned on like light bulbs – instantaneously – while women heat up slowly like irons. Amusing statements like this oversimplify the complexity and variety in human sexual relations – and may be hurtful to the many men who find they are *not* like light bulbs! Indeed there are many couples in which it is the woman who has the higher sex drive.

There have been many famous sex surveys, notably the ones conducted by Masters and Johnson, Kinsey and Hite. One common finding is that men reach the peak of sexual activity early on in life, usually in their teens, when they average five orgasms a week. By their forties this figure falls to two or three orgasms a week

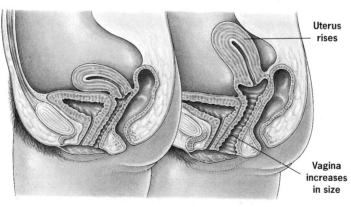

Uterus rises

Vagina increases in size

Female sex organs before (left) and during (right) sexual arousal.

and continues to decline with increasing age.

In contrast, women do not seem to reach their peak till their late twenties or thirties onwards, with a much steadier pattern of increasing and decreasing sexual activity, with increasing age, than seen in men. Women also have more complicated sexual lives, with the issues of menstruation, fertility, pregnancy and menopause playing important roles.

All surveys reveal that despite a 'general pattern' many individuals are very different from the average – and so, just as there are men who have not ejaculated for years, there are women who become aroused many times a day. Similarly there are men who ejaculate several times a day, and women who have only been aroused several times in their lives. The truth is, of course, that conforming to a 'general pattern' matters much less than being comfortable with one's own sexuality.

People's religious and cultural beliefs are hugely important in determining their attitudes to sex, and to what they feel is acceptable behaviour or not. Even if mentally they know that an activity (such as masturbation) is harmless, emotionally they may still feel guilt and regret.

A generation or so ago it was assumed that men were naturally more interested in sex than women and, as a result, overt behaviour such as masturbation, initiating sexual liaisons or even paying for sex was tolerated more in men than in women. The tide of feminism, and the recognition of women's rights and issues, have meant that the taboo around female sexuality has been lifted, and it is clear that sex is as important to women as it is to men. Women are now more able to admit to sexual appetites, and to masturbation and fantasy. In 1981 one survey found that 73 per cent of women interviewed said they had masturbated by the age of 20. The same researchers had done a similar survey 15 years earlier, and in 1966 the figure was only 46 per cent. Are more women masturbating now, or are they simply more able to talk about it?

HOW OFTEN DO OTHER COUPLES MAKE LOVE?

Most surveys have found that average frequencies of two or three times a week are common for most age groups. In general, however, sexual activity is higher in young couples, and couples who live together and are not married, and tends to decline after two years in both married and cohabiting couples. In some religions and cultures, sex during a woman's period is forbidden. In most couples, events such as pregnancy, child-rearing, family problems or work stresses alter sexual frequency. One well-known agony aunt claims that if, in the first five years of being together, a couple put a penny in a jar each time they made love, then after five years took a penny *out* each time they made love, the jar would never empty, even if they were together for the rest of their lives!

IS THERE MORE THAN ONE TYPE OF ORGASM FOR A WOMAN?

There has been much debate about the different types of orgasm a woman can have, with a suggestion that orgasms achieved through vaginal penetration only are more 'matured' than clitoral orgasms. Surveys have revealed, however, that most women are unable to have an orgasm without some clitoral stimulation before or during intercourse. It now appears that the female orgasm originates from the clitoris whether it is directly stimulated (by stroking or kissing) or indirectly stimulated (by penile thrusting).

Another controversy surrounds the existence or non-existence of the 'G-spot' – an area located

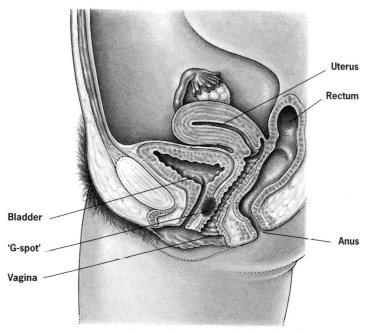

Some women find stimulation of the 'G-spot' highly arousing.

in the vagina just behind the clitoris. Some women find stimulation of this area highly arousing. It is thought that pressure on this area stimulates either the clitoris or the urethra indirectly, and is therefore pleasurable and exciting.

All these issues aside, the truth is that female sexual arousal is more complex and less obvious than the male response and most women take time to learn what their bodies like, and what is possible in conventional sexual positions and with each new partner. Most couples, if they are willing to experiment and communicate, will find a pattern of behaviour that satisfies them both.

WHAT CAN ONE DO WITH MISMATCHED SEXUAL DRIVES?

Few couples have perfectly matched sex drives and it seems unreasonable to expect one partner to feel as sexy and passionate as the other every time. This may have appeared to have been the case early on in the relationship, but most couples settle down to a frequency that takes into account their own sex drives, work, children, etc. If sex drives are really mismatched, it is helpful to talk about this fully and admit to this without any suggestion of failure or abnormality in either partner. In any sexual relationship the emphasis should be less on achieving orgasm and more on the closeness and communication that sex allows. Cuddling and stroking each other can be just as pleasurable as intercourse, and masturbation either by the partner or alone can take the edge off any frustration for the more active partner. If there is a serious difference in the amount or degree of physical intimacy each partner wants, then they may have to reassess their relationship to see if other positive factors make it worth maintaining.

KEY POINTS

✓ Physical changes during sexual arousal facilitate intercourse in most women

✓ Partners may differ in how quickly they become aroused

✓ Partners may differ in how often they want to make love

✓ Closeness and intimacy can be as fulfilling as intercourse

How problems begin

THE VICIOUS CYCLE

In almost every case of sexual difficulty, the patient's distress and fear of failure will aggravate the problem, even if the problem began purely as a physical one.

The newly delivered mother, with the tender vaginal scar, may start to tense up at the very thought of sex, because her first attempt after the delivery was so painful, and brought back to her all the trauma surrounding the delivery. The middle-aged man whose erection has failed twice in a row, perhaps because of overwork or too much alcohol, will treat his next attempt at intercourse as a personal challenge: 'If I can't do it next time I don't know what I'm going to do.' The pressure to perform becomes unreasonably high, the fear of failure is foremost in their minds, they fail to relax during intercourse and of course it happens again. The woman finds sex unbearably painful because she is so tense, and the man's erection fails. They both now really believe that they have a serious problem and a vicious cycle takes hold.

This vicious cycle can be surprisingly difficult to break, even if one understands what is happening. It is very easy to become locked in to feelings of self-doubt and low self-esteem, which become reinforced each time one 'fails' sexually. An understanding partner helps, but often the partner is also experiencing his or her own crisis of self-worth: 'Why doesn't he or she want to have sex with me anymore? Am I no longer attractive? Is he or she having an affair?'

An important part of sex therapy is therefore aimed at allowing couples to express these negative feelings, to pull themselves out of this downward spiral and to learn to enjoy physical closeness without performance pressure. 'Sensate focus' exercises, described later in this book (see pages 36–9) are used commonly by therapists to help couples slowly regain the relaxation, pleasure and confidence they once enjoyed.

IGNORANCE, MYTHS AND STEREOTYPES

Despite the greater availability of information these days, many people are still not very knowledgeable about many aspects of sex – from anatomy (especially female anatomy) to aspects of fertility, to the proper way to roll on a condom. Most people pick up bits of information along the way from friends or magazines, but this information is not always accurate.

Doctors quite commonly see women whose partners complain that they can feel a 'lump' in their vaginas during intercourse. An examination reveals that this lump is actually the cervix – which is a normal part of the body. Women in particular may grow up quite ignorant of their own genital anatomy. If they attempt intercourse and fail to allow penetration, they may think they are deformed, and are unable to believe that their vaginas *are* able to accommodate the erect penis.

Some people are also naturally shy and inhibited about sex. This may also be a result of their culture, religion or upbringing. Many religions, for instance, have strict rules about when intercourse can take place, what a woman can and cannot do while menstruating, and may forbid the use of contraception. The value placed on modesty may prevent a woman from examining and exploring herself, and make it extremely difficult for her to seek medical information or help. The association of sex with sin and guilt may be deeply ingrained and difficult to rationalise, and lead to various forms of sexual distress.

Another problem is that, despite a more liberal outlook, men and women are still expected to conform, in some way, to sexual stereotypes. Men are supposed to be highly virile, ready for sex at any time, powerful and in control of all aspects of their lives. They are *not* expected to be sensual, to give way to emotion, or to communicate easily their innermost feelings.

Women, on the other hand, receive the message that somehow sex and female genitalia are 'dirty', and that good girls do not seek or enjoy sexual release. Even leaving aside the fear that their signals will be misconstrued and perhaps lead to danger, many women find it difficult to be truly sexually expressive. Although it seems to be acceptable – even expected – for boys and men to masturbate, female masturbation and sexual fantasy are still taboo subjects.

These conflicting roles and expectations may add spice to the courtship stages of a relationship, but can be an obstacle to a fulfilling sex life in a longer partnership. Sex therapy allows individuals and couples to explore

their own feelings in relation to these complex cultural expectations. It may also give them 'permission' to be as sexual or asexual as they really want to be.

SEXUAL TECHNIQUE

Finally a word on technique. It is usually easier for a man to show a woman how he enjoys having his penis stroked than for a woman to explain how he should stimulate her clitoris. This requires a great deal more subtlety and unless the woman masturbates or has explored herself she may not know how she likes to be touched, or how to bring herself to orgasm. The clitoris is highly sensitive, and clumsy or heavy movement can be more painful than arousing. Most women find the tip is too sensitive to direct touch, and prefer the sides to be gently stroked.

It takes time in any relationship for two people to 'gel' sexually, and this is particularly so if either or both are sexually inexperienced. Good sex is usually a blend of passion, affection, abandonment and technique – none of which is easy to come by after a day at work. There are now plenty of sex manuals on sale in bookshops, and even videos with real couples. These may offer pointers for the less inhibited, but probably the best solution is to take time out with each other.

KEY POINTS

✓ It is easy to label oneself a 'sexual failure'

✓ Performance pressure ruins good sex

✓ Ignorance, misinformation and sexual stereotyping can cause sexual problems

✓ As far as sexual technique goes, practice makes perfect

When sex is painful

Painful sex is more common in women. The cause may be physical or psychological, and is often a combination of the two. A painful experience of sex may lead to anxiety the next time, poor relaxation and lubrication, and so sex is painful again, and so on. If anxiety is great, the vaginal muscles may go into spasm, blocking penile entry completely. This is called vaginismus, and is fully discussed below (see page 30).

Painful sex in men usually has a physical cause – commonly a skin infection of some sort on the skin of the penis. Other rarer causes are discussed below.

PAINFUL SEX IN WOMEN

The medical term 'dyspareunia' describes the condition when intercourse is painful, but possible. It is very common, and most women will have had at least some experience of it during their sexual lives. It is one of the most common complaints women make when they consult a gynaecologist, or a doctor in a sexual health clinic.

Occasionally a woman may be too shy to mention it and hope the doctor brings it up (which they may or may not do), or complain instead about another symptom, such as heavy periods. This is unfortunate, as the symptom of painful sex, if it occurs, can be helpful to doctors trying to reach a diagnosis.

CAUSES OF DYSPAREUNIA

Doctors divide dyspareunia into two categories: superficial or deep.

If the pain occurs when the penis enters the vagina, and is concentrated around the entrance to the vagina, it is called superficial dyspareunia. If the penis can be inserted comfortably but the pain occurs 'deep' in the lower abdomen, when the penis is fully

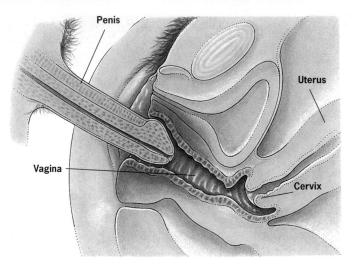

Superficial dyspareunia: pain concentrated around the entrance to the vagina.

inserted, it is called deep dyspareunia. Both may occur together.

If penile entry is impossible because the vaginal muscles go into a painful spasm, it is called vaginismus.

Common causes of dyspareunia include those in the box on page 27.

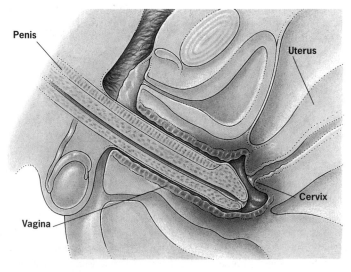

Deep dyspareunia: pain occurs when the penis is fully inserted.

CAUSES OF DYSPAREUNIA

Possible cause	Where is the pain felt?	
	Superficial	**Deep**
Infections	✓	✓
Postnatal or postsurgical problems	✓	✓
Problems with the cervix, uterus, tubes or ovaries	✗	✓
Insufficient lubrication	✓	✗
Having sex for the first time	✓	✓
Problems with the structure of the vagina or hymen	✓	✗
Psychological causes	✓	✓

● **Infections (superficial or deep):** Thrush (candida), trichomoniasis, genital herpes and low-grade bacterial infections are common causes of painful sex. Symptoms can include:

● A change in the colour, smell and amount of vaginal discharge

● Itching or pain

● The appearance of blisters or pimples, which may burst and discharge clear fluid, blood or pus.

Other infections, such as infection caused by chlamydia and gonorrhoea, are less common, but can lead to inflammation of the cervix and the pelvic organs, causing deep dyspareunia.

If an infection is suspected, a full check-up at a sexual health clinic (sexually transmitted infection/STI or special clinic) will be necessary. The appropriate treatment can then be prescribed.

As a general rule it is best to avoid washing the genital area with anything other than water because soaps, shower gels, bubble baths and disinfectants strip the vagina of healthy bacteria and allow other forms of infection to take hold.

Sex may be painful for a while even after the infection has cleared, because of remaining inflammation and reduced lubrication.

- **Postnatal or postsurgical problems (superficial or deep):** The shape of the vagina may be altered after giving birth, particularly if the vagina was torn or cut, and then stitched. The scar that forms may not stretch as much as the rest of the vagina, making sex painful.

Women can resume intercourse after birth as soon as they wish, and as soon as tears or episiotomies have healed. Some women resume as early as two weeks after delivery, although others prefer to wait till their first postnatal check. Women may find their libido changed (either increased or decreased) and that sex feels quite different compared to before they were pregnant, because of the stretching of the vaginal muscles.

The vaginal area may also be affected by operations for incontinence or vaginal prolapse. In some cases it may be possible for the surgeon to refashion scarred areas to allow for easier intercourse.

- **Problems with the cervix, uterus, tubes or ovaries (deep):** The following common gynaecological conditions can all cause deep pain on intercourse:

- Pelvic inflammatory disease (an inflammation of the uterus and tubes caused by infection).

- Fibroids: these are fibrous growths in the uterus. They may be single or multiple and cause pain as they increase in size.

- Endometriosis (the growth of uterine tissue *outside* the uterus, which also bleeds during periods).

- Ovarian cysts: these may grow progressively larger, and pressure during intercourse leads to pain.

Associated problems may include heavy, painful or irregular periods. If symptoms also include bleeding between periods or after intercourse, or lower abdominal pain and weight loss, tumours of the cervix or pelvic organs need to be ruled out.

Women should always be up to date with their cervical smears, and go to their GP for examination and investigation. A referral for an ultrasound scan and a gynaecological opinion may be necessary.

- **Insufficient lubrication (superficial):** Women who have prolonged or vigorous intercourse or frequent intercourse (several times daily) may suffer pain during sex simply as a result of friction. Lubrication with a water-based lubricant (e.g. KY Jelly) can help ease this problem, but it may be an idea to

A water-based lubricant can make sex more comfortable.

cut down on sex till it feels more comfortable. Remember also that oil-based lubricants (such as massage oils, Vaseline, cooking oil, etc.) can damage rubber and lead to condom accidents.

Women also vary greatly in the amount of lubrication they produce, even when sexually excited, and again the use of additional lubrication can make sex more comfortable.

Vaginal dryness and thinning of vaginal tissue is one effect of the menopause. Menopausal women should therefore use additional lubrication or consider hormone replacement therapy either locally to the vagina or for the whole body.

● **Having sex for the first time (superficial and/or deep):** Women having sex for the first time can find the experience painful, especially if the hymen has not been previously broken by tampons or other instruments. This is compounded by anxiety, lack of experience (of both partners), lack of arousal and therefore lubrication, and clumsiness or forcefulness by the male partner.

Anxiety can be dealt with by the following:

● Having sufficient information about the sexual act

● Being prepared beforehand for the prevention of pregnancy and sexually transmitted infections (with a condom and the oral contraceptive pill for instance)

● Being relaxed with one's surroundings and one's partner

● Making sure there is plenty of lubrication before penile entry is attempted.

Lubricants (e.g. KY Jelly, from the pharmacist) can be used safely with condoms. Most oils (cooking oil, massage oil, Vaseline) break condoms.

It may help if penetration is attempted slowly, in stages, with the introduction of one finger, and then two, beforehand. It may take several episodes of intercourse for the woman to relax fully and become used to the sensation of having her vagina stretched by the penis.

● **Problems with the structure of the vagina or hymen (superficial):** Some women have a particularly small vaginal opening, which becomes painful when stretched. In other women the hymen, which is normally torn during first intercourse, is stiff, and does not tear completely, giving rise to pain. Or it may split on two sides, leaving a hard band in the middle, which again makes sex uncomfortable. A few women have a 'septate vagina', in which their vagina is divided lengthways with a partition of tissue – this can of course lead to painful intercourse.

A physical examination by a doctor will rule out these unusual shapes, and in most cases simple surgery will rectify the problem.

● **Psychological causes:** As sex for women involves penetration, it is often important that it takes place in an atmosphere of relaxation and trust. Any anxiety (about their own sexuality, pregnancy, the relationship, etc.) can lead to tensing of the vaginal muscles and painful intercourse.

The woman may also become tense in response to a physical cause of pain, or a remembered trauma, e.g. childbirth or rape. Severe anxiety can lead to vaginismus which is discussed below. If a psychological cause is suspected, relationship or psychosexual counselling may be useful.

Vaginismus

Vaginismus is defined as uncontrollable tightening of the lower vaginal muscles, so that attempted penile entry is painful and impossible. In some cases the thigh muscles clench as well, so that the partner is unable to get near the vagina.

Vaginismus can range from the ability to use tampons and tolerate a vaginal examination but not to have sex, to the inability to touch or insert anything into the vagina without provoking the reaction.

Vaginismus is the most common cause of non-consummation of marriage and is thought to occur in about five of every thousand women, and makes up between 5 and 42 per cent of the sex therapist's workload.

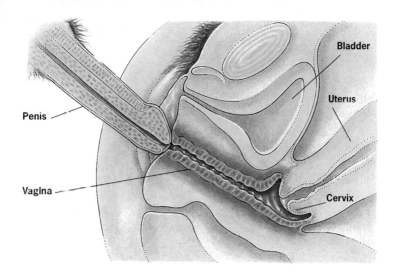

Vaginismus is an uncontrollable tightening of the lower vaginal muscles.

Vaginismus may be caused by any of the reasons for painful sex listed above, if pain and anxiety are severe enough. It may occur after a traumatic experience of sex, such as rape or sexual abuse.

In cases where there are no obvious precipitants, and the woman has not experienced intercourse, vaginismus is usually the result of uncertainty and misinformation about the sexual act and about female genitalia. There may also be deeply held religious beliefs or the guilty view that sex and nakedness are 'dirty'.

Vaginismus is best treated with the help of an understanding GP or a sex therapist.

A gentle examination is required to rule out physical problems.

Once this has been done, the woman is encouraged to express her fears or fantasies about her body, proceeding to an exploration of her own genitalia. Her partner may be present if she so wishes.

Once she is aware of which muscles tense and how to relax them, the therapist will demonstrate that gentle insertion of a finger is possible. The woman is then encouraged to explore her vagina with her own fingers, or with 'vaginal trainers' of different sizes. The couple may then proceed to exercises in which the woman controls penile penetration, before full intercourse.

The outlook is extremely good, and sex therapists find this a rewarding condition to treat. In mild cases, only a few visits may be necessary, but in severe cases more sessions may be needed.

PAINFUL SEX IN MEN

Painful sex in men is almost always related to a physical cause – psychological problems lead instead to difficulties with erection. Common causes include the following.

Trauma

Vigorous or prolonged intercourse can cause small tears in the foreskin and head of the penis (glans). Infection will make these more inflamed and painful.

Tight foreskin

Some men have difficulty retracting their foreskins, and erection may lead to tightness and discomfort. It may also be difficult to clean the area behind the foreskin, and any resulting infection will add to the problem. Circumcision should be considered if problems are frequent.

An occasional complication of a tight foreskin is called paraphimosis – in which the man is unable to bring the foreskin down again after erection. The foreskin forms a tight band around the penis, which swells and becomes painful. It is important to go to an accident and emergency department immediately in these cases, because permanent damage can result if the condition is left unseen to.

Infections and skin reactions

Herpes infection causes painful, itchy blisters on the penis, which burst after a few days and scab over. Warts look like tiny cauliflowers on the skin.

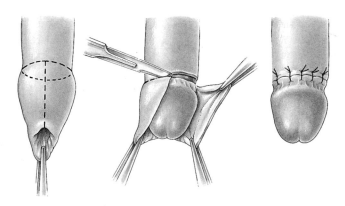

Circumcision is a minor operation that removes the foreskin.

Men can also get thrush, most commonly if their partners have it, and this causes irritation with redness and occasionally swelling at the head of the penis. A thick white discharge may collect underneath the foreskin.

Gonorrhoea and non-specific urethritis can cause both a burning sensation in the urethra with discharge, and pain on urination and ejaculation. If any of these infections are suspected, a full check-up at a sexual health clinic is necessary.

Some men are allergic to the rubber or lubricant used in ordinary condoms. Hypoallergenic condoms are now available from leading brands. It is also possible to react to massage oils, washing powders, shower gels or soaps.

Less common causes

Congenital deformities that cause bending of the penis with erection can cause pain. In a condition known as Peyronie's disease, a lump of fibrous tissue develops along the shaft of the penis, and causes a painful asymmetrical erection. The condition may resolve by itself over months or years, but help should be sought if intercourse is impossible. Surgery is the answer for some men. In both cases the opinion of a urologist may be helpful.

Some men develop great sensitivity in the glans of the penis after ejaculating, which can be so severe that the man fears to do it. Young men also sometimes have an over-active cremaster muscle (the muscle that causes the scrotum to contract) and this can produce spasmodic pain during sex. A long period of arousal without ejaculation can also produce an aching sensation in the groin.

Priapism is a condition in which the erection fails to subside and lasts for hours, becoming painful. Urgent treatment at an accident and emergency department should be sought, because permanent damage can result.

KEY POINTS

✓ If sex is painful, mention it to the doctor

✓ For women, painful sex may be superficial, deep or both

✓ Causes of painful sex in women are physical or psychological

✓ Vaginismus (preventing penile entry) can be overcome with the help of a sex therapist

✓ In men, painful sex is usually caused by a skin problem

Premature ejaculation (coming too soon)

Most young men, at the start of their sexual lives, 'come' quickly during intercourse, and this is probably a normal part of their sexual learning experience. Being highly sexed and easily aroused, they may be unable to hold off an orgasm until the female partner is also on the brink of one.

With experience and practice, many couples can find ways of having intercourse that satisfies them both; this may involve foreplay until the woman is sufficiently aroused, before penetration takes place, or frequent masturbation by the man to take the edge off his sex drive.

With increasing age, some men find that controlling their orgasm becomes steadily easier. But others find they continue to come too quickly, for both their own and their partner's satisfaction. In fact they may reach orgasm even before penetration, or only a few seconds afterwards. Prolonged sexual union is thus impossible, which damages intimacy between the partners and may threaten the relationship itself. The man may feel depressed and inadequate, and this can sometimes lead to other sexual problems, such as failure of erection or loss of sexual desire. The woman also suffers, feeling undesirable and unloved.

Premature ejaculation, or coming too quickly, is best defined as 'persistent or recurrent ejaculation with minimal sexual stimulation before, upon or shortly after penetration, and before the person wishes it'.

It is said to be the most common of all sexual difficulties. Studies have found that up to one-third of the general population reported difficulty controlling orgasm on a regular basis. Up to 60 per cent of men entering sex therapy have this problem.

First stage: sensate focus 1

1. Aim to make unpressured time for these sessions about three times a week. Try to ensure that you will not be disturbed – take the phone off the hook. Make sure you are warm enough and comfortable, and remove all clothing.

2 Make a strict agreement between you that, in the early stages of treatment, genital contact and intercourse are not permitted. This removes all pressure to perform or be aroused, and allows proper relaxation.

3. One partner lies back and relaxes while the other plays an active role, touching and caressing the other anywhere except the genitals and breasts. The person caressing should be assertive, exploring areas that they may never have touched before. The person being caressed should relax and aim at focusing on the sensation of being caressed. If they do not like what is being done to them, they should protect themselves by moving their partner's hand elsewhere.

4. The person being caressed should be aware of 'spectatoring', i.e. watching him- or herself being caressed in a detached way, rather than participating fully in it. This commonly happens, but becomes easier as relaxation occurs and the strangeness of the situation wears off. Relaxation and abandonment are the keys.

5. Try not to talk very much, and use non-verbal cues to communicate. The person being caressed can let his partner know what he likes or dislikes by removing the hand, putting his own hand on his partner's to increase or

decrease pressure, or change the pattern of touch, grunt or murmur words of encouragement and approval. He should not take charge, however, and should basically remain in the receiving role.

6. Take turns. If a session results in sexual arousal, masturbation is permitted but each partner should masturbate themselves and not each other.

Second stage: sensate focus 2

1. When you are both comfortable with the first stage, move to the second stage which is similar to the first except that this time breast and genital touching and kissing are allowed.

2 Put all the patterns of communication you established in the first stage to good use. With genital contact, small changes in pressure or direction can have a large effect.

3. Although the person who is being caressed may become aroused and even climax, orgasm is not the aim of the exercise, and the session need not end simply because of orgasm. Do not worry if something that felt good yesterday doesn't bring pleasure today – it is normal for body sensitivity to vary from day to day. Again, beware of 'spectatoring'. Relax and enjoy the sensations.

4. Massage oils and lubricants can be used to enhance the pleasure, especially when touching the genital areas.

Third stage: stop–start or squeeze

1. This stage deals specifically with premature ejaculation. After mutual pleasuring as described above (but before the man has had an orgasm) the man lies on his back and relaxes while the woman stimulates his penis till he is at the point of orgasm. At his signal, she stops stimulating him, until the urge to climax recedes. She then starts stimulating him again.

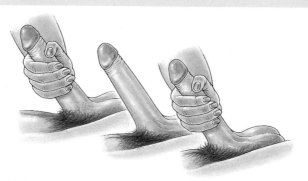

1. Stimulate to point of climax.

2. Stop stimulation until urge to climax passes.

3. Continue stimulation.

Stop–start technique.

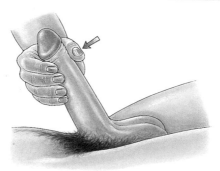

When orgasm is imminent, exert a firm pressure in a band, where the head of the penis joins the shaft.

Squeeze technique.

2. Instead of just stopping when orgasm is imminent, she may also employ the 'squeeze' technique, by grasping the head and shaft of the penis with her whole hand, the thumb and first two fingers exerting pressure on the area where the head joins the shaft. She maintains this pressure for 15–20 seconds, and then starts stimulating him again.

3. This process is repeated three times before the man is allowed to reach orgasm the fourth time.

4. Later, the use of a lubricant to simulate vaginal lubrication may be introduced.

Fourth stage: vaginal penetration

1. After touching and caressing as above, the woman sits astride the man and gently inserts his penis into her vagina. At first she does not move, but simply allows her partner to feel and enjoy the sensation of this. If he is close to orgasm she removes his penis and waits, or squeezes it as described above.

2 Once the man has become used to this sensation, the woman may move slowly with his penis inside her, again stopping if he is close to orgasm.

3. The next step is for the man to thrust, stopping and starting according to how he feels. He should, by now, fully recognise the sensations he has before orgasm, and have found ways to control this.

4. The man may slow or modify his thrusts instead of stopping, as better control is achieved.

5. The couple may proceed to full intercourse, using the principles that they have learned and adapting them as they wish.

Other surveys have found that about four per cent of men ejaculate within one minute of entering the vagina, and 75 per cent within two minutes.

WHAT CAUSES PREMATURE EJACULATION?

There are many theories about this. Some believe that early sexual experience in hurried circumstances, i.e. in the back of a car or if there is a danger of discovery, trains a man to ejaculate quickly.

Others feel that anxiety is the cause, or excessive sensitivity to erotic stimulation.

The well-known sexologist Helen Singer Kaplan believes the root of the problem lies in the man's inability to recognise, and therefore control, the sensations that occur just before orgasm, and many sex therapists endorse this theory. She compares it to a child learning how to hold urine – which the child cannot achieve until he recognises,

becomes used to and gains control over what it feels like to have a full bladder.

Physical causes are very rare, although if a man has had no problem previously and no change in circumstance (i.e. a new partner), prostate or neurological disease needs to be excluded by a doctor.

TREATMENT

For some men, using a condom to lower sensation can make the difference. An anaesthetic gel (such as lidocaine) on the penis may also make ejaculation easier to control. This is available at chemists without a prescription.

Standard treatment involves sex therapy, although drug treatment is also available. Researchers have found that newer antidepressants (such as Sertraline) can delay ejaculation and increase satisfaction for both patient and partner. Intermittent use seems as effective as continuous use. Side effects, however, may include nausea and lowered libido.

Sex therapy for most cases of premature ejaculation is successful, sometimes within weeks, but requires good communication between partners and a disciplined approach.

Enlisting the aid of a sex therapist is helpful for many couples, because it is easier to follow a set programme, and certain 'do's and don'ts', if these are spelled out by a figure of 'authority' outside the relationship.

A sex therapist can also educate the couple about their sexuality, help to explore and release the anxiety or acrimony that may have accumulated around the issue, and provide encouragement and support. Occasionally, the therapist may recommend relationship counselling before the problem of premature ejaculation is tackled.

However, if both partners are well motivated and basically at ease with their sexuality, and the relationship has not suffered as a consequence of this condition, it is perfectly possible to follow the series of exercises at home.

What treatment involves

Most therapists use a combination of 'sensate focus' followed by the 'stop–start' technique, or the 'squeeze' technique.

Sensate focus is a method developed by the famous sexologists Masters and Johnson, and is designed to allow the couple to rediscover the pleasures of simply touching and stroking each other in a relaxing way, without pressure to become aroused or reach orgasm, and therefore removing the anxiety to perform.

For many couples, their feelings about sex will have become too focused on orgasm, and their ability or inability to give each other pleasure. Sensate focus provides a way for the couple to start all over again.

In the stop–start technique, the woman masturbates the man till he is near orgasm and, at his signal, she stops till he feels the urge to reach orgasm diminish. She then starts stimulating him again, and the process is repeated several times before he is allowed to reach orgasm. In the squeeze technique, the woman squeezes the penis at the point of orgasm for 15–20 seconds, until the urge to reach orgasm is lost and the erection diminishes slightly. Again the process is repeated several times before orgasm is allowed.

These two techniques work, because they familiarise the man with the sensations just before orgasm and, in a step-wise manner, allow him to gain control over them. Some men find that once they learn the control they keep it; others may have to repeat the exercise at certain intervals.

It should be stressed that the general principle of sex as a method of relaxation and mutual pleasuring, and not simply as a vehicle for orgasm, is a good one to keep in all relationships. The exercise described may need to be repeated at intervals over the following months.

The success rate is excellent, with therapists reporting a greater than 90 per cent 'cure' after 3–4 months.

KEY POINTS

✓ Ejaculation control often improves with age and experience

✓ Premature ejaculation is the most common sexual problem

✓ Sensate focus exercises help a couple renew their intimacy

✓ 'Stop–start' or 'squeeze' techniques can help a man gain ejaculatory control

✓ Success rates for premature ejaculation are very high

Problems with erection

Most men have had the occasional, embarrassing experience of badly timed erection failure – tiredness, alcohol and the pressure to impress a new partner are often to blame.

It is estimated, however, that up to five million men in the UK have persistent problems with erection. Other surveys have found that about seven per cent of all men will experience serious problems with their erection at some point in their lives.

Unfortunately data also suggest that only ten per cent of those who have problems seek treatment, which can be successful in many cases.

Many men may choose instead to ignore or deny the situation, often at great cost to their own happiness and the stability of their relationship. A man who has erectile problems can feel deeply inadequate and unmanly, and avoid sexual contact with his partner.

His partner may also suffer, feeling helpless and rejected, or wonder if he is having an affair.

'Erectile dysfunction' is the modern term to describe persistent problems with erection. It replaces the older, still widely used term 'impotence', which is inaccurate because of its connotations of weakness or unmanliness.

Erectile dysfunction can range from the ability to achieve erection and orgasm by masturbation but not intercourse, to the total inability to achieve erection, no matter how stimulated.

Experts now believe that in about 70 per cent of cases there is a physical cause, with psychological causes accounting for the remainder.

Successful treatment is available for both causes. If a man still has the occasional erection *at any time*, e.g. in sleep or first thing on waking, his problem is almost certainly psychological.

CAUSES OF ERECTILE DYSFUNCTION
Physical causes

- **Alcohol and drugs:** Alcohol consumption is thought to account for one in six cases of erectile dysfunction. Prescribed drugs can also cause problems, and these include some antihypertensive medications (methyldopa, guanethidine, beta blockers and diuretics), drugs containing the female hormone oestrogen, or drugs that counteract the male hormone testosterone. Cocaine can also decrease erection.

- **Conditions that affect hormone levels:** Conditions that affect the organs that regulate hormone levels in the body can have an effect on erection. These include Addison's disease, adrenal gland tumours, rare conditions affecting testosterone production, obesity, and overactive or underactive thyroid.

- **Conditions affecting the circulation:** An erection requires blood to flow into the penis, and to remain there and not 'leak' out. If this mechanism is affected either way, i.e. too little blood in or too much blood out, erection can be affected. Blockage of the blood supply to the penis (similar to blockage of the heart vessels in heart disease) is a common cause. Heavy smokers are therefore at risk of both, and of poor circulation elsewhere in the body.

- **Diabetes:** Diabetes can cause blood vessel disease, and can also affect the nerve supply to various parts of the body, including the penis.

- **Neurological conditions:** These include conditions that affect the spinal cord or nerve supply to the penis, such as spinal injury, multiple sclerosis or tumours. Surgery to the prostate may rarely cause problems due to nerve or tissue damage.

- **Conditions affecting the penis itself:** Conditions affecting the tissues of the penis lead to difficulties with erection. These include Peyronie's disease (fibrous swelling of part of the penis), damage caused by untreated priapism or paraphimosis (see page 32) or infection.

- **Serious illness:** Severe, chronic disease of the liver or kidneys may lead to erectile failure. Any serious illness (heart attack, heart failure, chest problems, injury, major surgery) can result in erectile dysfunction for a variety of reasons.

Psychological causes

Any psychological stress or disturbance can interfere with erection. People who are depressed, anxious or traumatised by a recent event can experience erectile failure. Relationship problems or marital discord can also manifest itself this way. Men who are confused about their sexual orientation may be unable to achieve erection with a female partner. The pressure to perform sexually can also lead to failure, and up to a quarter of men who seek help for erection difficulties originally had problems with premature ejaculation.

TREATMENT

Treatment is very much tailored to the cause. A man with erectile problems may seek help through a variety of sources – general practitioners and sexual health clinics (genitourinary or special clinics) are good initial points of contact. Referral to a specialist in a variety of disciplines (hormones, diabetes, circulation, etc.) may then follow.

Age should not be a barrier to seeking help; although erectile problems are more common in older men, they should not be seen as a fact of ageing. The doctor will need to ask about the patient's medical and sexual background. He or she may then ask more specific questions about the pattern of erection difficulty, and about any other emotional or relationship difficulties that may be present.

Initial tests may include a full medical examination, a blood pressure check, and a series of blood and urine tests. Further investigation will depend on what the doctor finds.

- Changing lifestyle or medication
- Drugs: Viagra
- Injections
- Vacuum devices
- Surgery
- Medication
- Penile implants

Treatment options for physical causes of erectile dysfunction

- **Changing lifestyle or medication:** Cutting down or stopping alcohol intake and smoking can help a great deal. A change of medication, if options are available, may do the same.

- **Drugs:** A few years ago Viagra was hailed as a wonder drug offering a solution to erectile dysfunction that could previously only have been dreamt of. In recent years, several new drugs have become available and the choice includes the following:

- Viagra is a trade name for a drug called sildenafil. It works by blocking an enzyme, which in turn prevents the blood vessels in the penis from filling. The final effect is that, with sexual stimulation, the blood vessels are able to fill to a greater extent and so the erection is harder.

Taken an hour before intercourse, seven out of ten men achieve an erection when stimulated and aroused; in this way it has a far more natural effect than some therapies which give an erection no matter what the circumstances. Improvements have been seen in both physical and psychological causes of erectile dysfunction, although men with diabetes or those who have had prostate surgery report less success.

Side effects are uncommon but include headache, skin flushing, dizziness and diarrhoea; more importantly, the drug can be dangerous for men with certain heart conditions, so it is crucial that it is obtained through the proper channels and prescribed by a doctor.

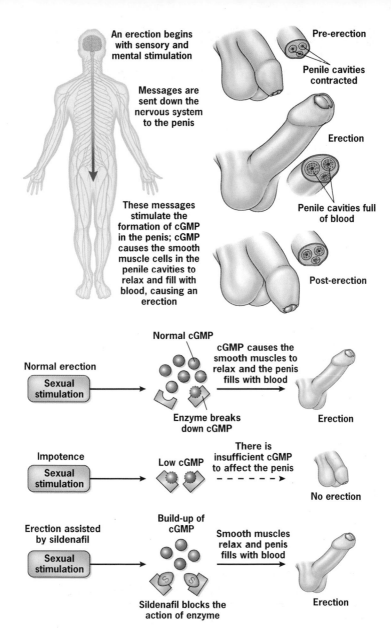

An erection begins with sensory and mental stimulation

Messages are sent down the nervous system to the penis

These messages stimulate the formation of cGMP in the penis; cGMP causes the smooth muscle cells in the penile cavities to relax and fill with blood, causing an erection

Pre-erection

Penile cavities contracted

Erection

Penile cavities full of blood

Post-erection

Normal erection

Sexual stimulation

Normal cGMP

Enzyme breaks down cGMP

cGMP causes the smooth muscles to relax and the penis fills with blood

Erection

Impotence

Sexual stimulation

Low cGMP

There is insufficient cGMP to affect the penis

No erection

Erection assisted by sildenafil

Sexual stimulation

Build-up of cGMP

Sildenafil blocks the action of enzyme

Smooth muscles relax and penis fills with blood

Erection

Sildenafil, and similar medications, help to restore natural erectile function in the presence of sexual stimulation.

- Cialis (tadalafil) and Levitra (vardenafil) are drugs that have a similar action to Viagra. Although there are many similarities between these drugs, they differ in dose and for how long they stay effective. For example, although Viagra and Levitra can aid erection for up to four hours, Cialis continues doing so for 24 hours or more.

- Apomorphine is a drug that works by stimulating certain receptors in the brain, especially in an area called the hypothalamus. This results in a relaxation of penile muscle, which increases blood flow into the penis, thus improving erection. It is given in a tablet dissolved under the tongue about 20 minutes before sex, and works for about three hours. It does not work if the tablet is swallowed. Side effects include headache, yawning, nausea and dizziness.

All these drugs have potential side effects and may interact with existing medical conditions and therapies. They should be prescribed only by a doctor who has details of the patient's overall health. The choice of drug depends on the medical advice and personal preference.

In rare cases hormone therapy may be suitable. Some men also find the drug yohimbine helps increase penile sensitivity and aids erection. The drug is, however, unlicensed for this use, and can only be prescribed if the patient pays for it. It should also not be taken by patients with heart conditions or high blood pressure.

- **Injections:** In this method, the man learns to give himself a small injection into the penis before intercourse takes place. The erection occurs within 10 minutes and lasts a sufficient length of time for sex (about 45 minutes) and will subside of its own accord. This method is popular among many men, because results are quick and the injection can be done discreetly. If needles are a problem, a treatment in which the drug is introduced into the urethra as a small pellet may be suitable. This is known as MUSE (medicated urethral system for erection). The rare side effect to watch out for is priapism – when the erection lasts for longer than four hours. This needs to be reduced in a hospital accident and emergency department urgently or permanent damage may result. The dosage then needs to be adjusted to avoid this again.

- **Vacuum devices:** This involves the man putting his penis into a plastic cylinder, which is then pumped to create a vacuum. This results in an erection, which is maintained by a rubber band at the base of the penis. This is also a popular method and good if needles are unacceptable. The process can be seen as being rather mechanical and unromantic, but otherwise works very well. The rubber band can be used on its own in some men who are able to achieve an erection but not to maintain it for intercourse.

- **Surgery:** This can help men whose specific problem is blood flow to the penis. Surgery may be able to remove any blockage that prevents an erection, or repair any leakage of blood from the penis during erection.

- **Penile implants:** Inflatable or semi-rigid rods can be surgically placed along the shaft of the penis. With the semi-rigid rods, the erection is present all the time. The inflatable device is more sophisticated and is connected to a pumping device usually placed in the scrotum. Surgery is usually seen as a last resort, but many men who have had this operation are pleased with the results.

Psychological treatment

Psychosexual therapy or relationship counselling can address emotional issues which may have led to erection failure. This can be done alone or with the partner.

In general terms the man has to recognise that his unhappiness, fear or anxiety about a certain issue is responsible for his erection problem, and that the therapist is not going to 'teach' him how to regain his erection. A man cannot will an erection any more than his female partner can will vaginal lubrication. He often also needs to recognise that his anxiety about his erection has led him to become a 'spectator' sexually, i.e. in lovemaking, he watches anxiously over his performance, rather than give himself over to pleasurable sensations.

Once the therapist has explored various issues, the couple may be set exercises to re-learn pleasuring each other in a completely non-threatening way. These usually include sensate focus (see page 36) with the emphasis in later stages on the man maintaining his erection.

The outlook for those who are well motivated is excellent, and most men benefit from treatment whether for physical or psychological causes.

KEY POINTS

✓ Seventy per cent of cases of erectile dysfunction have a physical cause

✓ If erection can occur spontaneously at any time, the cause is likely to be psychological

✓ Age should not prevent anyone from seeking help

✓ A variety of treatment methods is available

✓ The outlook for many men is excellent

Problems with orgasm

The general impression that men have far fewer problems reaching orgasm than women is supported by statistics. Various surveys have estimated that, although only about one to four per cent of the general population of men have trouble with orgasm, the figure is up to 40 per cent for women.

Up to 26 per cent of women report that they never achieve orgasm through intercourse, and up to 80 per cent are able to achieve orgasm during intercourse only 'with assistance', i.e. foreplay involving clitoral stimulation.

Sex therapists have largely come round to the idea that it is actually 'normal' for a woman to have trouble reaching orgasm without clitoral stimulation. However, about 10 per cent of women never reach orgasm by any means.

In the same way that young men need to learn to *control* orgasm, young women often have to learn how to achieve one.

Although female masturbation is still widely considered less acceptable than male masturbation, many women learn about how they like to be stimulated by touching themselves. Once they know what they like, it becomes much easier to communicate their needs to their sexual partner.

Even if a woman knows how to bring herself to orgasm, many positions adopted in sexual intercourse do not provide sufficient clitoral stimulation for the woman to orgasm. The process may therefore have to be 're-learned' with each new partner, and couples need to take their time to work out a pattern of foreplay that satisfies them both.

CAUSES OF FAILURE TO REACH ORGASM

In all cases, poor technique and inadequate stimulation may be the main problem.

Physical causes

A little alcohol can be relaxing, but too much has a deadening effect on sexual performance. Men may find it harder to maintain an erection, whereas women find it harder to become properly aroused to climax.

Drugs, prescribed or otherwise, may also have this effect, and any drug that lowers libido (sexual urge) can also inhibit orgasm. Drugs include cocaine, barbiturates, thioridazine, some medications for high blood pressure, oestrogens, antidepressants and occasionally the oral contraceptive pill.

Surgery can also interfere with sexual satisfaction, although in many cases the cause is more psychological than physical, i.e. resulting from a reaction to mastectomy, colostomy or genital surgery. There is some evidence that hysterectomy can lead to less satisfactory orgasm in some women. Prostate surgery decreases sexual functioning in only a small proportion of men.

Any serious or long-term illness can lead to lowered sexual urge and difficulty with orgasm. Painful intercourse, for whatever cause (see pages 25–34), may make a person too tense and anxious to achieve orgasm. Only in rare instances is the failure to have an orgasm caused by a neurological problem.

Psychological causes

Orgasm is a reflex that occurs when there has been enough sexual stimulation for the person to reach 'the point of no return'. Getting enough stimulation for long enough may be the main problem, especially for women, but other factors can make it harder to reach that 'point'.

Women especially need to feel secure and relaxed before they can abandon themselves to sexual arousal. Unresolved worries about pregnancy, the relationship, etc. can interfere with excitement.

If orgasm has not been achieved several times, performance anxiety and fear of failure make the problem worse, and a pattern of behaviour called 'spectatoring' can take hold. Instead of allowing their bodies simply to enjoy erotic sensations, the importance of reaching orgasm means that the person is always asking herself: 'Is this how I'm meant to feel? Am I near orgasm yet? Why not? What's wrong?' This kind of anxiety clearly dampens arousal and inhibits orgasm.

Studies of women who are unable to have an orgasm also reveal a variety of other factors – fear of loss of control, competitive or aggressive feelings, unrealistic worries about urinating if they have an orgasm, etc. These should be explored further with a psychosexual therapist.

TREATMENT FOR DIFFICULTIES WITH ORGASM

This is best discussed with a psychosexual therapist, who can help decide what the basic problem is. If it is one of sexual technique, the therapist can help the couple explore new ways of stimulating each other, and perhaps teach the woman exercises to maximise clitoral stimulation during intercourse. In other cases the emphasis may be more on psychological issues.

If 'spectatoring' is a problem, the therapist may encourage distraction by fantasy, aided if necessary by erotic literature or film, and sex aids such as vibrators. Specific exercises to help a man or woman achieve orgasm may include the steps in the box on page 54.

When the use of fantasy is second nature, the vicious cycle of anxiety and fear of failure, leading to 'spectatoring', will hopefully be broken.

OUTLOOK

The outlook for failure of orgasm is usually very good, with sex therapists quoting success rates of around 90 per cent within 20 sessions.

A STEP-BY-STEP GUIDE TO OVERCOME 'SPECTATORING'

1. Self-stimulation with fantasy, alone

2. Self-stimulation as above, but with the partner present; initially the partner can be present but with his or her back turned

3. Mutual pleasuring, using sensate focus exercises (see pages 36–9)

4. Mutual foreplay to orgasm, without intercourse, again using fantasy and distraction

5. Full intercourse

KEY POINTS

✓ Women have more problems reaching orgasm than men

✓ Masturbation is an important way for women to learn what they like

✓ Failure to reach orgasm may have physical and psychological causes

✓ Fantasy and self-stimulation are good ways to overcome 'spectatoring'

Low sex drive

Sexual desire (or libido) is similar in many ways to an appetite for food.

When we are feeling happy, healthy and carefree, we tend to enjoy food more and consequently eat more. If we are tired, stressed and anxious we lose our taste for food, and may even lose weight as a result.

For both men and women, the feelings of relaxation and well-being are important to the ability to enjoy sex, and so life events (marriage, house moves, new baby, new job, etc.) can dampen sexual desire.

Most people recover their stride once the 'crisis' is past. If they are unable to, it may be that more serious problems, perhaps with the relationship itself, need to be resolved.

Less common are those who have rarely or never been sexually aroused, who never masturbate or fantasise about sex, and who seem disinterested in engaging in a sexual relationship. They may be perfectly comfortable with themselves, or seek help because they feel that they are 'different' from the rest of the population.

Low sex drive may be *global,* that is, the person is unable to feel aroused in all situations and with all partners, or it may be a problem only with a certain partner or in certain situations. Whatever the case, as with many other sex problems, low sex drive can be the result of physical illness, drugs or psychological conflict.

Sex therapists estimate that about 40 per cent of people who seek their help come because they are worried about having a low sex drive. However, individual sex drive varies so much that it is not always easy to say what is 'low' and what is 'normal'.

In men, sexual activity peaks in the late teens, when they are intensely interested in sex, and thereafter slowly declines, so that in adulthood and middle age they are able to go for longer and longer periods without release, and not experience frustration. They can, however, become highly sexually active again when attracted and excited by a partner.

Women experience a more gradual rise in interest in sex, which peaks in their thirties. It appears that their sex drives are more fragile and easily dampened, compared with those of men, although they have the capacity to have more orgasms.

A young man who shows little or no interest in sex and rarely masturbates and a 39-year-old woman who cannot be aroused by herself or any partner are therefore different from the normal experience, and can be said to have low sex drives.

CAUSES OF LOW SEX DRIVE
Physical causes

- **'Normal':** Just as we accept some people have large appetites for food or drink, it is clear from sex surveys that libido varies hugely in the general population. All surveys report on men and women who reach orgasm several times a day on a regular basis, and also those who go for long periods without seeking sexual release.

- **Hormonal:** A sudden change in libido, with no other obvious factors, may rarely indicate disease of the hypothalamus, pituitary gland or the testicles. Otherwise, in men, the level of the male hormone testosterone decreases with increasing age, and some men may find their libido tailing off earlier than others. Women, whose sex drives are more fragile, may also notice fluctuations during their monthly cycles, and experience large changes with major hormonal events, that is, pregnancy, after childbirth, menopause. Women taking hormonal therapy of any sort, including the oral contraceptive pill, may also find their libido affected.

- **General health:** Not surprisingly, serious illness or chronic health problems can sap libido, partly due to stress but also perhaps due to specific biochemical causes. Loss of sex drive may also be a feature of postviral fatigue.

- **Drugs:** Many drugs can lower libido. Among these are drugs used to treat schizophrenia or psychotic states, morphine-based pain killers, beta blockers for hypertension and hormone therapy as mentioned above. Men who take oestrogens or cyproterone acetate will find their libido diminished.

- **Mood changes:** Sexual appetite can be the first thing to go in depression – before loss of appetite for food, or inability to sleep. Conversely, people who are manic and hyperactive have greatly increased sex drives. The fragility of an individual's sex drive to fluctuations in mood varies, so it may appear that relatively small events can still have a large impact for some people.

Psychological causes

It is important to differentiate between the loss of sexual interest in one's partner, through tensions within that relationship, and the loss of sexual desire itself. It may be easier to complain of a low sex drive than to admit that one partner has simply 'gone off' the other, or that for some reason sex with that partner creates too much anxiety. In such cases, the desire itself may be intact, but suppressed – or the person may find release through masturbation or other partners.

Other reasons why a person may lack sexual desire can be complex and very individual, and need to be explored carefully. For some people, sex is too closely related to fear and anxiety or guilt and shame, to the point that they are unable to become aroused. Others may find their own sexual fantasies alarming – perhaps if they involve homosexuality or violence or unusual practices – and are therefore fearful of their sexual identities.

Some people find that they are only able to feel sexually aroused in situations that are 'safe' to them, i.e. with strangers, prostitutes, etc., and the possibility of a committed relationship with a compatible partner represents too much 'danger'. They may have found the partner of their dreams, and desperately want a committed relationship, but are at a loss to explain why they cannot be sexually aroused by them.

TREATMENT AND OUTCOME

As the causes of low sex drive are so varied and can be so complex, the length of treatment required and how successful it is also vary a great deal. Clearly someone with a well-defined problem which can be resolved quickly will do better than someone whose situation is more complex.

In some cases, relationship counselling is more appropriate for couples who have normal individual sex drives but who are having problems relating to each other sexually. Otherwise, psychosexual therapists may see a person on his or her own or a couple together. They may use a variety of treatment methods, but the main objective is to help the person or couple gain insight into *why* they have gone off sex. This may be combined with simple, nonthreatening sexual exercises (see pages 36–9) or erotic tasks to carry out at home, and the feelings around these tasks are explored.

Soon after Viagra hit the headlines as a cure for erectile dysfunction in men, news reports suggested it was also a wonder drug for women who had problems with sexual arousal and orgasm. Viagra for women is marketed as a cream (called Viacreme) on the internet. Although Viagra may increase genital blood flow in women the same way it does in men, clinicians have cautioned that sexual arousal for women (and probably men) has more to do with psychological and emotional factors than blood flow changes. Some women with specific problems with physical arousal may find it helpful, but many others may not.

As some of the psychological issues relating to low sex drive can be highly complicated, therapy for some cases needs to be lengthy and intense before any improvement is seen. Although many people can be helped, a few will remain difficult to treat.

KEY POINTS

✓ It may be normal to have a low sex drive

✓ Low sex drive must be differentiated from relationship difficulties

✓ Some psychological causes are deeply complex

✓ The outcome depends on the cause and whether it can be resolved

Special circumstances

In this chapter, the effects of major events and illnesses are briefly outlined. In the case of operations, the surgery may affect the functioning of the sex organs and/or be seen as 'mutilating'. After serious illness, such as a heart attack, the fear that sex could provoke another serious setback can be completely inhibiting. Although more information about particular conditions should be available from the specialists involved, psychologists and psychosexual counsellors would also be able to offer support and treatment in most cases.

SEX DURING PREGNANCY

Many women experience changes in libido during pregnancy. Several surveys have found that the general pattern seems to be a lowering of sexual interest in the first and last three months of pregnancy, with, occasionally, an increase in libido during the middle three months. It is difficult to tell whether the massive hormonal changes that take place during pregnancy, or the social and emotional adjustments that are necessary, are responsible.

It used to be thought that sex and orgasm during pregnancy were possibly harmful to the fetus, and therefore to be avoided. More recent research indicates that this is mostly untrue. Occasionally, women who have had problems at varying stages of their previous pregnancies may be advised to avoid intercourse at that particular time. For instance, if a woman had previously miscarried during the second three months of her pregnancy, due to a relaxed cervix, she may be advised to abstain from sex at this time, the next time round.

The mechanics of having sex during pregnancy, especially in the later stages, calls for some agility and experimentation! It may be difficult to hold each other front to front, never mind try to have sex this way. Possibilities include the woman-on-top position, or entry from the rear, or variations of side-by-side positions. Oral sex and mutual masturbation are also good options.

Men may find the body changes that accompany pregnancy highly arousing or perhaps off-putting. In particular, the vagina feels different, being softer and wetter. There is also a heavier vaginal discharge. Pregnancy is often both a joyful and a stressful time for a couple, and both partners may feel differently about sex at different times. Spending intimate time with each other cuddling and stroking, and offering sexual release, with or without intercourse, can provide the reassurance that both partners may need.

SEX AFTER CHILDBIRTH

Surveys have found that most women have resumed having sex by 12 weeks after giving birth, with about a third having done so by 6 weeks. The quality of sex after childbirth is influenced by many things. Both partners may be tired and distracted by their new role as parents. The woman may have had stitches in the vagina, which occasionally cause continuing problems with painful sex. A traumatic experience of childbirth can also lead to vaginismus (see page 30).

After a vaginal delivery, the vagina may feel more lax, and grip the penis less tightly. Pelvic floor exercises can help the woman regain her vaginal tone.

Breast-feeding can also have an effect on a couple's sex life.

Full-time breast-feeding is a tiring, time-consuming business, and the woman may be too tired, from interrupted sleep, to enjoy sex. There is some controversy as to whether breast-feeding raises or lowers a woman's libido. The hormonal levels of a breast-feeding mother may suggest that her libido may be lowered, but some women find breast-feeding an erotic experience. Men have different reactions to watching their partners breast-feed, and some men find it upsetting.

Generally, most couples find that they have sex less than they did before their child was born.

SEX AFTER SURGERY
Prostate operations

Enlargement of the prostate is a common complaint in middle-aged and elderly men, and it is often assumed that any operation in this area will lead to impotence or problems with erection. The most common method of operating on the prostate is through the urethra – the so-called transurethral resection of the prostate (TURP) – and in good hands this only results in erection problems in five per cent of cases. Surgery and radiation treatment for prostate cancer, on the other hand, carry higher risks of erectile dysfunction. After a standard prostatectomy, about 80 per cent of men develop erectile

difficulties, and recent studies have shown that radiation treatment results in similar rates. However, in a technique known as nerve-sparing prostatectomy, more than 80 per cent of men regained or maintained their erections 18 months after the operation.

Some centres are also performing nerve-grafting techniques, which have good results in preserving erections. However, the type of surgery required to treat the cancer varies from case to case and problems with erection may not be avoidable.

Many men will find, however, that, even if their ability to have an erection or to reach orgasm is not disturbed, they do not ejaculate semen as they did before. Instead, the semen is directed into the bladder. This is known as retrograde ejaculation. This does mean that the man is likely to be infertile, although sperm collected from the urine immediately after orgasm has been successfully used to artificially inseminate a partner.

If surgery is for prostatic cancer, other methods of treatment such as oestrogens, drugs that counteract the male hormone testosterone and removal of the testicles may be necessary. This is because the prostate cancer depends on testosterone for growth. The result of these treatments is likely to be a lowering of libido.

Hysterectomy

It is still unclear whether the uterus is important for orgasm. Some studies have found that women's sexual satisfaction increased after hysterectomy, others that it deteriorated. Many women report no change.

If removal of the uterus is accompanied by the removal of both ovaries, then there may be hormonal reasons why libido may decrease. Otherwise many women feel released from the problems that they were suffering before the operation (for instance heavy, prolonged and painful bleeding) and embark on a new, enthusiastic phase in their sexual lives.

Mastectomy

About a third of women who have undergone a mastectomy find that, temporarily at least, their enjoyment of sex is reduced. Mastectomy brings a massive alteration to body image, and some women imagine that they are sexually deformed, and no longer attractive. Women may receive advice after the operation on breast reconstruction and breast prostheses, and it is important that the sexual repercussions of the operation are not forgotten by partners or counsellors.

Bowel surgery

Major bowel surgery sometimes involves the bringing of one bit of bowel out to the exterior – this is called an ileostomy if the small bowel is involved, or a colostomy if the large bowel is involved. A bag is placed over the bowel opening to hold the bowel contents. Understandably this kind of operation can have a large psychological effect and interfere with a person's sexual functioning.

On top of this, some surgery can also damage the nerve supply to the genitals, and cause sexual problems in this way. This is much more common if the rectum (the back passage) has been removed. In such cases, about a third of men suffer erectile problems, and a third of women find sex painful because of scarring in the area. It has been known, however, for sexual function to improve over several years after the operation.

People who have an ileostomy or colostomy may be haunted by anxieties that new partners may find their bodies off-putting, that their regular partners may reject them sexually, that the bag will burst during lovemaking, or release unpleasant sounds and smells. Clearly, time to adjust and sensitive handling on the part of new or established partners, or counsellors, will help. Many people get married and have children after such operations. The couple may have to find new ways of lovemaking that

they both find acceptable and pleasurable.

SEX AFTER A HEART ATTACK

Sex should be seen as part of 'getting back to normal' after a heart attack. Unless there are major complications following the attack (in which case the person is likely to be too unwell to think about sex), there are no special reasons not to have sex. The exertion involved in sex is said to be similar to that of climbing two flights of stairs – and if this is possible, then so is relaxed, non-athletic intercourse.

Occasionally sex provokes angina. A glyceryl trinitrate (GTN) tablet or spray can be taken before-hand. Sometimes treatment for high blood pressure is started after a heart attack. Certain blood pressure medication, such as diuretics and beta blockers, can occasionally cause erectile problems or loss of libido. If this happens, consult the doctor for a change of dose or medication.

SEX AFTER A STROKE

One survey of male stroke patients found that, for most of them, sexual interest and erections reappeared within seven weeks of the stroke. A person may be left partially paralysed or weak on one side after a stroke, and so sex has to be modified to take this into account. As with heart attacks, new medication may sometimes affect sexual functioning, and it would be wise to check this out with the doctor.

SEX AFTER SPINAL INJURY

The actor Christopher Reeve may have caused some surprise when he announced, only months after the injury that left him paralysed from the neck downwards, that his libido was very much intact, and that he hoped one day to father another child.

Although individual cases need to be considered separately, the evidence seems to be that many men and women who have spinal injuries and are paralysed have normal sexual appetites. Some men become impotent after the injury, but many do not. Ejaculation is affected more than erection. Even if there is no feeling in the genitals, many paraplegic individuals describe the ability to have orgasms, which are different from the orgasms they had before their injury.

Women seem to be less affected than men, and many adjust to a new and pleasurable sex life. Fertility in women is often unaffected, and women continue to menstruate as before. Men may become infertile, depending on whether they are able to ejaculate, but artificial insemination is sometimes an option.

For more information, contact SPOD (Sexual Problems of the Disabled), 286 Camden Road, London N7 0BJ. Tel.: 020 7607 8851.

KEY POINTS

✓ Pregnancy may affect libido either way

✓ For a variety of reasons, a couple's sex life may be different after a child is born

✓ The impact of major surgery on the sexual functioning of the patient should never be forgotten

✓ Sex is part of getting better after a stroke or heart attack

✓ People with spinal injuries may continue to enjoy rewarding sex lives

Teenagers and sex

Erotic thoughts, intense interest in all matters sexual, deep anxieties about one's body, confusion about what one is doing (compared with what everyone else seems to be doing) and feeling trapped between parents' warnings and bodily urges: the teenage sexual experience can be both as intensely exciting, and as fraught with guilt, anxiety and complication, as the adult experience. However, the unwanted consequences of sex – sexual infection and pregnancy – are far harsher for the teenager than for the adult.

Teenagers nowadays may appear more streetwise than their

parents did at a similar age, but the greater social pressures to perform sexually may mean that adolescence is an even more bewildering experience. Currently the teenage pregnancy rate in Britain is about 40,000 a year. This is the highest in western Europe and six times the rate in the Netherlands. A recent nationwide sex survey revealed that about a fifth of men, and more than two-thirds of women, felt they had started having sexual intercourse too early. The average age for losing one's virginity is now 17. By age 15, a quarter of teenagers claim to have had sex.

Many teenagers may feel that intercourse is a long way off, but be preoccupied with related issues such as masturbation, menstruation, nocturnal emissions and confusion over their own sexual orientation. Clear and independent information from reliable sources such as family planning clinics and the Brook Advisory Centres (specially for young people) is valuable, because the adults closest to the confused teenager can sometimes provide conflicting advice.

MASTURBATION

Masturbation – touching one's own genitals for pleasure and orgasm – is widely accepted as natural in teenage boys, but many teenage girls masturbate too, and continue to do so throughout womanhood. In teenagers masturbation is a useful way to discover sexual pleasure and release, safely and privately, and can help determine one's preferences during foreplay in later sexual activities. It can also help reveal one's own potential for orgasm.

Boys masturbate by rubbing their penises along the shaft and the glans, either with their hand or against a surface, e.g. the bed. Girls may gently stimulate their clitoris with small repeated movements, and touch their vagina and breasts. There is no 'normal' frequency for masturbation – some people masturbate several times a day, others once a week or less often. It is also perfectly natural not to want to masturbate.

It used to be thought that masturbation was unnatural and even harmful, possibly causing blindness. Now it is known as the safest form of sex, and is a perfectly normal behaviour that many adults enjoy throughout their lives.

HOMOSEXUAL FEELINGS

Adolescence is commonly a time of heightened emotion, and many teenagers develop passionate friendships and deep feelings for people they admire of either sex. Many teenagers become fixated with members of the same sex, and may be confused about whether they are homosexual (attracted to the same sex) or heterosexual (attracted to the opposite sex). Teenagers may also experiment sexually with a same-sex partner. All this is perfectly natural, and part of discovering one's own sexuality.

Many people who had homosexual feelings and experiences go on to forge heterosexual relationships later on. Others feel strongly that they are attracted to the same sex, and maintain this preference throughout their lives. Still others are able to be attracted by either sex, although they may maintain a stable relationship with one person. If a person has relationships with both sexes he or she may refer to him- or herself as 'bisexual'.

Many societies emphasise the family unit and tend to view heterosexual relationships as normal, and homosexual partnerships as abnormal, sinful or deviant. The pressure to conform to a heterosexual world is therefore very powerful. The truth, however, is that for most people sexuality is a spectrum – they may prefer to have sex with the opposite sex, but in some circumstances may be attracted to the same sex, and vice versa.

Many homosexuals say that they knew from a very young age that they were 'gay'. If someone is confused about their sexuality, they should allow themselves time to consider things carefully. Some people try to deny their sexuality to the point of getting married and having children, but this often results in greater unhappiness. Living as a homosexual can bring much conflict and complication, but it may be better to be honest about it.

HEAVY PETTING

It is normal to be curious about sex and to try things out. Many young couples experiment with sex by kissing, kissing with tongues, and perhaps feeling each other's bodies through their clothes. Heavy petting generally refers to removing clothes and touching each other's body, and perhaps masturbating each other. It is the same as 'foreplay' before intercourse, and can lead to intercourse.

It is important therefore, if you are to enjoy experimentation, to establish right from the start what the limits are for both partners. No one should pressurise the other into taking petting or kissing a step further if they are unwilling to do so, no matter how 'carried away' you are. If petting leads to intercourse, the question of condom use for the prevention of pregnancy and infection will have to be dealt with (see Contraception on page 69). It is also important to remember that semen should not be ejaculated near the vagina, as this can result in

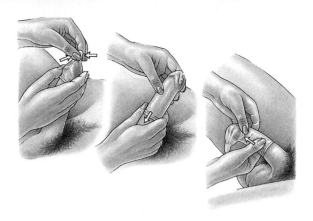

| 1. Squeeze teat to prevent air being trapped. | 2. Roll the condom the full length of the penis. | 3. After ejaculation, remove the condom carefully while the penis is still erect. Tie the condom off and throw in a bin. |

Make sure that you put the condom on properly.

pregnancy. Furthermore, infections can be spread if fingers that touch the genitals of one partner then touch the genitals of the other. To prevent infection, any cuts or broken skin on fingers should be covered with waterproof plasters, and male and female condoms can be worn. For safer oral sex, flavoured condoms are now available from chemists or family planning clinics.

If both partners accept and agree on the limits of their heavy petting, then this can be a very enjoyable and relatively safe way to enjoy sex without the complications of intercourse.

FIRST-TIME INTERCOURSE

Having intercourse for the first time is seen as an important rite of passage into the adult world. It is easy to rush into it without thinking it through properly. First-time sex between two experienced partners is often awkward and clumsy, simply because of the newness of the situation. If both partners are inexperienced, it can be even more difficult, as both are likely to be shy, nervous and anxious. It helps, therefore, to take time to get to know each other well, and to be at ease with each other's bodies. More importantly the issue of condom use and contraception should be agreed ahead of time. About 70–80 per cent of teenagers report that they used a condom the first time they had sex. As teenagers are likely to be highly fertile, it may be sensible for the girl to be on the Pill, and for the boy to use a condom against infection (see Contraception below).

PREGNANCY, CONTRACEPTION AND SEXUALLY TRANSMITTED INFECTIONS

Sexual intercourse may result in pregnancy or sexually transmitted Infections, or both. Both partners should take equal responsibility for making sure that neither occurs, and if an unwanted pregnancy does occur, they should take equal part in sorting out the situation. Family planning advice can be obtained from a variety of sources – family planning clinics, GP surgeries and Brook Advisory clinics, specially for young people. These provide fully confidential services – parents need not be told, although the young people may be encouraged to discuss their decisions with their parents. Family planning clinics also provide free condoms.

Many girls will opt to go on the contraceptive pill which has to be prescribed by a doctor. If taken properly this will provide good protection against pregnancy. To protect against sexual infections a condom should always be used each time as well. Condoms provide good protection against infections such as HIV, gonorrhoea, chlamydia and trichomoniasis – but must be put on before any genital contact is made. They provide some protection against warts and herpes.

If the girl is NOT on the pill, and sexual intercourse takes place without a condom, or if the condom bursts or slips off, **emergency contraception** can be taken to lower the risk of pregnancy up to **72 hours after the event** (the other name for emergency contraception is 'the morning-after pill' but this is inaccurate because it works for **three days** afterwards). This is now available at chemists without a prescription. It is also available at family planning clinics, some sexual health clinics, GP surgeries and accident and emergency departments. It consists of two tablets taken together in one dose and will reduce the risk of pregnancy down to about two per cent.

KEY POINTS

✓ Sexual feelings are normal

✓ Masturbation is the safest form of sex

✓ Homosexual feelings may be part of one's sexual orientation

✓ Partners should not put pressure on each other to start having sexual intercourse

✓ If you are going to have sexual intercourse, be informed and prepared to prevent pregnancy and sexual infections

A quick word about safer sex

No book on sex nowadays is complete without some advice about keeping healthy and avoiding sexual infections, including HIV infection.

With the exceptions of gonorrhoea and trichomoniasis, the numbers of cases of other common sexual infections have shown significant increases in recent years. The incidence of genital warts, for instance, showed a 225 per cent increase in one recent ten-year period.

Sexual infections used to be synonymous with promiscuity and infidelity, but today this is no longer the case. For better or worse, it is now common for men and women to have several sexual partners before committing themselves to a long-term relationship (marital or otherwise) and some infections are legacies of previous encounters.

Many couples now take the opportunity to have a full check-up for sexually transmitted diseases, and possibly an HIV test, before either foregoing condom use or planning a family. The stigma previously attached to attending a sexual health clinic (genitourinary medicine clinic or special clinic) is now much less. Women also commonly use these clinics to seek help for minor gynaecological problems such as thrush or cystitis.

ARE CONDOMS REALLY NECESSARY?

The best method of avoiding most, although not all, sexual infections is to use a condom always, with every partner, and to put it on before there has been any genital contact. This will help prevent infections such as non-specific urethritis, chlamydia, gonorrhoea, trichomoniasis and HIV. It will give some protection against herpes and warts, but no protection against pubic lice.

Condom use becomes even more crucial if you are in a higher-risk situation – such as having sexual intercourse abroad, with prostitutes, male homosexuals or someone known to be an injecting drug user.

Some men find condoms difficult to use, and have problems maintaining an erection with one on. The female condom (Femidom), which is available at family planning clinics and at chemists, may then be a useful option.

GOOD HABITS

General hygiene is also important in sexual relationships. Women especially may find that they suffer sensitivity and irritation in less hygienic conditions. It is good practice to wash the genital area before and after sex, and for women to urinate soon after intercourse, to prevent cystitis.

It is *not* a good idea, however, to go overboard about washing, and sensitivity to soaps, bath additives, deodorants and douches is a common problem. Women are generally advised to avoid bubble baths and douches of any sort (especially disinfectants) because they strip away the normal bacteria in the vagina, which leaves room for other bacteria to move in. This can lead to thrush or a condition called bacterial vaginosis, which causes a creamy discharge with a fishy smell. Washing regularly with water only should be sufficient.

WHAT ARE THE COMMON SYMPTOMS?

It has to be remembered that many sexual infections can remain undetected because they cause such mild symptoms that the person does not notice them. Some infections are notorious for remaining hidden – chlamydia infection in women, for instance, is often noticed only when it has caused further complications such as tubal damage leading to infertility or pelvic inflammatory disease.

Discharge and discomfort

Men may notice a pus-like discharge from their urethra, and women may notice a change in their normal vaginal discharge. It may be heavier or have a different colour or smell from normal. Men may also notice pain when they urinate, or a burning irritation down along the penis. Women may have irritation round the vagina, painful intercourse or stinging when they urinate.

These symptoms may be caused by non-specific urethritis, gonorrhoea, chlamydia, trichomoniasis or thrush.

Skin ulceration

The most common cause of painful skin ulceration or blistering is herpes. Syphilis, a rare disease nowadays, causes a painless ulcer. Other causes of broken skin include severe thrush, or trauma through vigorous sex or inadequate lubrication.

Lumps, boils or warts

It is common for people to seek help about a growth on their genitals that they had not previously noticed. Sometimes these turn out to be pimples or boils, and sometimes they are warts, which require treatment. Women may get a swelling in the lower third of their vagina, on one side, caused by an infection of a gland called the Bartholin's gland. Treatment is not always necessary, but the swelling sometimes has to be cut and drained of pus.

Pelvic pain

Women may complain of severe periodic pain in the lower abdomen or in their sides, whereas men complain of pain in their pubic region, sometimes shooting to their testicles or penis. This can be caused by infection in the pelvic organs in women (pelvic inflammatory disease) and the prostate in men. It can be difficult to pinpoint the infection, however, and sometimes long courses of antibiotics are necessary. Such infection may be the result of untreated sexual infection such as gonorrhoea or chlamydia.

Itch

Men and women may complain of itch anywhere on the genitals or in the pubic hair. This can be caused by poor hygiene, thrush or pubic lice, or herpes. It is also possible for common skin problems such as eczema to affect the genitals.

HOW TO GET HELP

There are now 230 sexual health clinics in the UK. The best thing to do, if you suspect that you have an infection, is to attend a clinic for a full check-up and treatment, and advice about avoiding further problems. GPs are also available to help, but often do not have the full range of testing facilities.

Sexual health clinics offer a strictly confidential service, with separate hospital notes from the rest of the health service, and so nobody, not even your GP, can find out about your attendance unless you give your permission. Appointments may be necessary but you do not need to be referred by anyone else.

If you do have infection, your partner will also need to be tested and receive treatment. Untreated infection in sexual partners causes the spread of infection in the general population. Some infections may also damage the unborn fetus.

If both you and your partner are receiving antibiotic treatment, it is most important that you abstain from intercourse until you have both been given the all-clear by the clinic. Otherwise you may continue

to pass the partly treated infection back and forth and continue to have problems.

Many sexual health clinics also offer a comprehensive service with full-time counsellors, health advisers, psychologists or psychosexual therapists. These people provide useful advice and information about dealing with sexual problems, relationships and any unwanted effects of a sexual relationship – a pregnancy or an infection such as herpes. They also offer advice and support concerning HIV infection.

KEY POINTS

✓ Regular condom use cuts the risk of sexual infection significantly

✓ Good hygiene is important between partners

✓ Women should wash their genitals regularly with water only

✓ For a full confidential check-up, make an appointment with the local sexual health clinic

Useful information

Benefits Enquiry Line
Helpline: 0800 88 22 00
Website: www.dwp.gov.uk
Minicom: 0800 243355
N. Ireland: 0800 220674

Government agency giving information and advice on sickness and disability benefits for people with disabilities and their carers.

British Association for Sexual and Relationship Therapy
PO Box 13686
London SW20 9ZH
Tel: 020 8543 2707
Fax: 020 8543 2707
Email: info@basrt.org.uk
Website: www.basrt.org.uk

Supplies names of accredited local psychosexual therapists.

Brook Centres
Studio 421, Highgate Studios
53–79 Highgate Road
London NW5 1TL
Tel: 020 7284 6040
Fax: 020 7284 6050
Email: admin@brookcentres.org.uk
Helpline: 0800 018 5023
Website: www.brook.org.uk

Offers free, confidential helpline to young people aged up to 25 years on contraception, sexual health and personal relationships. Recorded information also available on 020 7617 8000.

Careline
Cardinal Heenan Centre
326–328 High Road
Ilford IG1 1QP
Tel: 020 8514 5444
Fax: 020 8478 7943

Helpline: 020 8514 1177
(Mon–Fri 10am–4pm, 7–10pm)
Website: www.carelineuk.org

Provides confidential crisis telephone counselling for children,
young people and adults on many
issues, including family, marital and
relationship problems.

Childline

Freepost NATN 1111
London E1 6BR
or
45 Folgate Street
London E1 6GL
Tel: 020 7650 3200
Fax: 020 7650 3201
Helpline: 0800 1111
Textphone 0800 400222
Email: info@childline.org.uk
Website: www.childline.org.uk

Confidential, free counselling
helpline for children and young
people in trouble or danger 24
hours a day, every day. Comforts,
advises and protects and, where a
child is in danger, works with other
helping agencies to ensure the
child's protection.

Family Planning Association

2–12 Pentonville Road
London N1 9FP
Tel: 020 7837 5432
Fax: 020 7837 3042
Helpline: 0845 310 1334
Website: www.fpa.org.uk

Offers telephone advice Mon–Fri
9am–6pm on contraception and
sexual health. Appointment needed
to view their reference library.

Family Planning Association Scotland

Unit 10, Firhill Business Centre
76 Firhill Road
Glasgow G20 7BA
Tel: 0141 576 5088
Fax: 0141 948 1172
Email: jackien@fpa.org.uk
Website: www.fpa.org.uk

Offers telephone advice on contraception and sexual health.

Family Planning Association Cymru

Canton House
435–451 Cowbridge Road East
Cardiff CF5 1JH
Tel: 029 2064 4034
Fax: 029 2064 4306
Email: fpacymru@fpa.org.uk
Website: www.fpa.org.uk

Offers telephone advice on contraception and sexual health.

Family Planning Association Northern Ireland

113 University Street
Belfast BT7 1HP
Tel: 028 9032 5488
Fax: 028 9031 2212
Email: belfast@fpani.org.uk
Website: www.fpa.org.uk

Offers telephone advice on contraception and sexual health as well as
unplanned pregnancy support.

London Lesbian and Gay Switchboard

PO Box 7324
London N1 9QS
Helpline: 020 7837 7324
Website: www.queery.org.uk

Offers 24-hour telephone information and advice on sexual health for parents and people who are, or think they are, gay, lesbian or bisexual.

London Marriage Guidance
76A New Cavendish Street
London W1G 9TE
Tel: 020 7580 1087
Fax: 020 7637 4546
Helpline: 0800 652 2342
Email: info@counselling4london.com
Website: www.counselling4london.com

Runs a counselling service for couples in London. Information leaflets available.

Men's Health Helpline
Medical Advisory Service
PO Box 3087
London W4 4ZP
Tel: 020 8995 8503
Fax: 020 8995 3275
Helpline: 020 8995 4448 (Mon 7–9pm)
Website:
www.medicaladvisoryservice.org.uk

Offers information on all aspects of men's health, including sexual problems such as premature ejaculation and erectile dysfunction. For written information an SAE is requested.

National Institute for Clinical Excellence (NICE)
MidCity Place
71 High Holborn
London WC1V 6NA
Tel: 020 7067 5800
Fax: 020 7067 5801
Email: nice@nice.nhs.uk
Website: www.nice.org.uk

Provides guidance on treatments

and care for people using the NHS in England and Wales. Patient information leaflets are available for each piece of guidance issued.

The Outsiders
BCM Box Outsiders
London WC1N 3XX
Tel: 020 7354 8291
Helpline: 0707 499 3527
(11am–7pm weekdays)
Email: info@outsiders.org.uk
Website: www.outsiders.org.uk

Offers information and can refer people to therapists who can help with sexual relationship problems. Puts people with similar sexual problems in touch with each other.

Relate National Marriage Guidance
National Office
Herbert Gray College
Little Church Street
Rugby
Warwickshire CV21 3AP
Tel: 01788 573241
Fax: 01788 535007
Helpline: 0845 130 4010
Email: enquiries@relate.org.uk
Website: www.relate.org.uk

Do not have counsellors on hand, but can refer you to one of 400 local branches. Relate publications available at bookshops, libraries or via website.

Sexual Dysfunction Association
(previously The Impotence Association)
Windmill Place Business Centre
2–4 Windmill Lane

Southall, Middx UB2 4NJ
Tel: 0870 774 3571
Email: info@sda.uk.net
Website: www.sda.uk.net

Runs an information helpline, publishes leaflets and advises on referral services in erectile dysfunction.

Sexual Health and National AIDS

Helpline: 0800 567123
Website: www.playingsafely.co.uk

Free Government helpline offering 24-hour confidential advice on HIV, AIDS and other sexually transmitted infections.

WEBSITE

BBC Health Website
www.bbc.co.uk/health/sex

Offers wide-ranging information on all aspects of health, including sexual problems.

THE INTERNET AS A SOURCE OF FURTHER INFORMATION

After reading this book, you may feel that you would like further information on the subject. One source is the internet and there are a great many websites with useful information about medical disorders, related charities and support groups. Some websites, however, have unhelpful and inaccurate information. Many are sponsored by commercial organ-

isations or raise revenue by advertising, but nevertheless aim to provide impartial and trustworthy health information. Others may be reputable but you should be aware that they may be biased in their recommendations. Remember that treatment advertised on international websites may not be available in the UK.

Unless you know the address of the specific website that you want to visit (for example, familydoctor. co.uk), you may find the following guidelines helpful when searching the internet.

There are several different sorts of websites that you can use to look for information, the main ones being search engines, directories and portals.

Search engines and directories
There are many search engines and directories that all use different algorithms (procedures for computation) to return different results when you do a search. Search engines use computer programs called spiders, which crawl the web on a daily basis to search individual pages within a site and then queue them ready for listing in their database.

Directories, however, consider a site as a whole and use the description and information that was provided with the site when it was submitted to the directory to decide whether a site matches the searcher's needs. For both there is little or no selection in terms of quality of information, although engines and directories do try to impose rules about decency and content. Popular search engines in the UK include:

> google.co.uk
> aol.co.uk
> msn.co.uk
> lycos.co.uk
> hotbot.co.uk
> overture.com
> ask.co.uk
> espotting.com
> looksmart.co.uk
> alltheweb.com
> uk.altavista.com

The two biggest directories are:

> yahoo.com
> dmoz.org

Portals

Portals are doorways to the internet that provide links to useful sites, news and other services, and may also provide search engine services (such as msn.co.uk). Many portals charge for putting their clients' sites high up in your list of search results. The quality of the websites listed depends on the selection criteria used in compiling the portal, although portals focused on a specific group, such as medical

information portals, may have more rigorous inclusion criteria than other searchable websites. Examples of medical portals can be found at:

> nhsdirect.nhs.uk
> patient.co.uk

Links to many British medical charities will be found at the Association of Medical Research Charities (www.amrc.org.uk) and Charity Choice (www.charitychoice.co.uk).

Search phrases

Be specific when entering a search phrase. Searching for information on 'cancer' could give astrological information as well as medical: 'lung cancer' would be a better choice. Either use the engine's advanced search feature and ask for the exact phrase, or put the phrase in quotes – 'lung cancer' – as this will link the words. Adding 'uk' to your search phrase will bring up mainly British websites, so a good search would be 'lung cancer' uk (don't include uk within the quotes).

Always remember that the internet is international and unregulated. Although it holds a wealth of invaluable information, individual websites may be biased, out of date or just plain wrong. Family Doctor Publications accepts no responsibility for the content of links published in their series.

Index